THE CHOICE AND COMMITMENT

Everything Starts and Ends With You

MEL B. COOK

DEDICATION

To my parents that allowed me to fail and make my own mistakes. There is absolutely no way I could've survived the ill ways of the world without your demonstration of tenacity, bravery, and strong work ethic.

CONTENTS

INTRODUCTION

Choosing to be great is a choice and choosing to put yourself first is a commitment. It is the most fulfilling commitment one could ever make, but throughout life's woes, we rarely remain faithful. We have to make a conscious effort to stay on track and check in with ourselves. It's important to regularly schedule alone time, connect to our core, complete tasks that make us happy, and continue to take deep breaths when we're overwhelmed.

Most of you reading this book are currently battling with something in your life. Don't feel alone. Life can be overwhelming and sometimes, it leaves us in distress. Whatever it is, it's not the end of the world. What happened the last time you felt like the world was ending? You survived and today will not be any different. Rejection sucks, people disappoint you, and things don't always go as planned. Nevertheless, you can control your will to be great in the face of adversity. It might wind you or wound you, but the victory is yours for the win.

Depression is a bitch. I wish I could refer to her using nicer terms but there is nothing nice about that bitch. One minute you can be floating through life, enjoying a beautiful run, and then a storm hits. Instantly, you have to focus on keeping all your balls in the air with the wind blowing at 90 mph. Instead of this bitch moving along and minding her business, she decides to become the liability in the middle of your misfortune. She is the gang leader that brings along all of her flunkies to her dirty work. So, not only do you have to deal with Depression, you have her cousins Doubt, Dismay, Fear, Anxiety, Resentment and all of the others showing up.

You're going to kill yourself if you try to deal with all of them at the same time. The easiest way to defeat them is by working on YOU. You have to focus on making you stronger, happier, resilient, and an all-around freakin' boss. Everything starts and ends with you. The road isn't easy but it's rewarding. There isn't anyone who deserves you more than you and there isn't a greater commitment that you can make to yourself. All were lessons I've learned along the way.

I had many moments in life that tried to define me but I couldn't allow that to happen. Instead, they became my stepping stones to becoming stronger and greater than ever before. I am a survivor of sexual assault. I experienced numerous losses at a very young age. I'm a product of a failed marriage and two parents that didn't have contact for decades. I've been ridiculed, criticized, and counted out. Then, there were times I was a statistic and times I've made myself a statistic. I've done a lot, I've seen a lot, and I've heard a lot. As a result, I've been suicidal and homicidal. However, through it, all grabbed onto what was working in my favor, and I never gave up.

The moment I realized greatness was a choice, my life changed forever. It began to shape my perception and left no room for excuses. It made me own every part of my life, myself, and my future. As a result, I've been able to achieve what folks thought was impossible and what continues to baffle the minds of many. I am not a doctor. I am a regular girl that has been through some shit and with tons of help, I learned how to talk myself off the ledge effectively. I learned how to win even when it feels like I'm losing. I don't speak on things that I never experienced, and I don't assume that everyone is the same. However, I know we all have similar struggles, and if we communicated more, then we wouldn't feel alone or like we were fucking crazy.

Throughout this book, we are going to go on a journey together. Explore alternative ways of thinking and ways we can evolve into the best version of ourselves. Anything you read is tried and true. I understand we are two different people and results may vary. However, thanks for allowing me to share my experiences, regimens, and methods. I am certain you will gain some insight that you can apply to your everyday life. Also, I know that everything starts and ends with you. Your consistency and commitment can take you to new heights where the possibilities are endless. If I can happily live my version of the American dream, then so can you.

BE NICE

*I*t is so easy to be overcritical and judgmental when you live in a society that consistently places you in a box and adores culturally specific packages. A society that values superficiality over integrity and authenticity, as if, we were all created one-dimensional and we're only useful in one area in life. It's hard to find your path, and it's hard to understand you can only be great on the path that was naturally designed for you. Often, the environment forces you to doubt who you are, what you are trying to accomplish, and your self-worth. Everyone assumes what role would best fit you and how you should act according to that role. You will not always live up to their expectations or your expectations of yourself. You will fall, you will fail, and your victories won't always be flawless, but no matter what you must be kind to yourself, Shit! You're human. Life is a journey. No matter your faults you are amazing and capable of amazing things.

Your life belongs to you. It's the one thing that isn't up for debate or dispute. Frequently, we forget it when we are journeying through life. Nonetheless, it doesn't make it less true. The decisions you make influence others, but they're your decisions to make. They may not always be the best decisions, but they're still yours. They may not shine the brightest light, but they're still yours. Your greatest decisions represent your greatest characteristics. However, your poor decisions test your character in unimaginable ways. As a result, you either learn from the mistakes, or you let the mistakes define you. If the latter happens, you'll constantly find yourself battling you. Also, questioning your entire being and your life's work. It will have you drowning in tears and sinking in self-pity. It won't make you work hard, try hard, or destined for greatness. It sucks the hope right out of you, and it makes waking up an arduous task.

There is a point in life when you have just to keep it moving. Commit to get over it and not sweat over things that's won't matter in the long run. You may not be ready to move on completely, but at least commit to trying. Forgive yourself for everything that hasn't gone right and everyone that has done you wrong. Its water under the bridge and you can't change what has already happened. It's done already, no matter how terrible it may have been and no matter how bad it made you feel. Some things were your fault, and some things were out of your control. We have all abandoned our common sense and earned a few T-shirts. Anyone who tells you differently is a liar. Don't be a liar and don't associate with liars.

I have spoken to many people across the U.S. that have questioned their identity and their purpose. Normally, the onset is sparked by a major life change, such as a death, break-up, divorce, childbirth, huge transition, or a major loss. At some point, we all have been there, and it sucks. More so, because when you are in a dark place it is a struggle to find light. You focus on all of the negatives and don't give yourself the credit that you deserve. You completely leave out the part of your story when you have overcome obstacles or lived to see another day. You get so caught up in the now that everything you survived is ignored. If you are going to tell the story, then tell it right and include everything. Make it a story about how you were a victor and not a victim. There is power in that story and power in telling that story, even if it's just to yourself.

Give yourself permission to breathe, heal, and grow. The only way that happens is if you learn not to be so hard on yourself and not to compare yourself to others. Do you think you're the only person that has been through some shit? You're not. Every pic you double click, status that you like, or person you follow has a story. Every person you come in contact with has gone through a questionable situation or experienced something they prefer is never revealed. You can see if someone has placed filters on a photo but not on their life. Therefore, don't deplete the value of your life trying to live up to someone else's image. Habitually, we negatively compare ourselves. Instead, let's use those comparisons to prove that we are human and capable of human things. I dare you to look at the bio of your favorite celebrity or public figure. You will find messages of their insecurities, struggles, and demons. Also, of persistence and tenacity. They may have 1 out of a million professions, but at the end of the day, we all have the same basic parts and minutes in a day.

Progression takes time and patience. It takes commitment and acknowledging that some things may need to be done differently. Some upsets are foreseen and unseen, so you can't escape them. As long as you dwell on the earth shit will happen. Consequently, you have to resist the urge to be self-demoralizing and supercritical, because neither are supportive of your development. I promise we will work on ways to create a process that encourages progression without living in the past. You are never alone, and you are never the only one, although sometimes it feels like it. We have all been messed up and messed over, but we can all make a choice to live or to die in it. It is your life, and you have full control of the impact each situation has on you. However, it doesn't have to define you. Everything starts and ends with you. Own it but remember to be kind to yourself.

Chapter Question:

To move forward in life, what three things require your forgiveness?

1. _____

2. _____

3. _____

Activity:

1. Get three helium balloons.

2. On each balloon write out an item from your list above.

3. Place the balloons in your hand and go outside.

4. Say, "I no longer give you the power to hold me back, make me feel guilty, or stop me from getting the life that I deserve. I am releasing you so that I can release me into the next chapter of my life."

5. Release the balloons.

Notes:

_____

_____

_____

_____

_____

_____

_____

_____

_____

_____

_____

_____

_____

_____

_____

_____

_____

_____

_____

CONTROL YOUR INTAKE

*E*verything you consume potentially impacts your decisions and choices. You'd be surprised what has harbored space in your mind and is waiting to come out. Waiting for the proper opportunity to surface and to define your moment. It is easier for us to accept and expect positive things to lurk but what about the negative stuff. The stuff that causes us to self-destruct and go off the handle and claim our losses. We want to minimize your chances of ghost and demons jumping out of the closet, which will not only scare you but everyone you encounter. That is why it is so important to control and monitor what you intake on a regular basis.

Most people dedicate their whole lives to winning, which is why they aren't prepared to take the losses. If you are one of those people, then let's change that today. We no longer want you to place yourself at great risk; to be blindsided and derailed from your greatness. A place where your hard work, achievements, and future goals are compromised. A place where the fibers that hold your family together unravel, your legacy unfolds, and you don't know how to pull it together.

The goal is not to have a loser mindset or to become

obsessed with losing. It's to make sure that a loss or series of losses doesn't permanently take you out the game by monitoring and controlling your intake. The only way to control a negative is to counteract it with a positive. That's why it's important for your brain to constantly snap positive images, listen to positive messages, and download positive thoughts. It serves as your first defense to fight off anything meant to destroy your self-image, self-esteem, and self-worth.

There isn't one person that wakes up and says, "I want to be a loser." On tough days, you may feel like a loser, but nobody wants to be a loser. Nobody wants that one loss to define them forever. However, one bad day can easily turn into 100, if you aren't careful. Winning is amazing. So amazing that most people don't prepare for the worst-case scenario. They don't consider what it takes to recover from life's unfortunate events and hurdles. They don't realize there is an art to bouncing back, which begins way before you take a loss. It's all about controlling and monitoring your intake on a regular basis because what we consume has a critical impact on our actions and decisions. You want to create a plan that promotes healthy living, affirms your purpose, and supports your goals.

Currently, what happens when life hits you with a horrific blow? Do you bounce to your feet or do you lay on the mat helpless; allowing your dreams to be stripped away with each breath? Truthfully, life's unexpected blows have stolen the promise and expectation of many. Therefore, the training doesn't start once you're hit. It should start the day you're born or at least once you realize a quality life is worth hard work and preparation.

Growing up, I was required to go to church three times

during the week and twice on Sunday. I hated it. I didn't understand many of the messages and I thought most of the people were hypocrites. When I grew older, I checked out and stopped attending church. Physically, I rejected everything spewed at me from the pulpit. Then one day, I had an unsettling feeling in my spirit. I grabbed the bible and placed it on my nightstand. It was the first time I picked up a bible in 3 years. Honestly, I don't even know why I picked it up because at the time I wasn't a believer. In the trouble-some hours of the night, I was awakened by my ex-boyfriend making a plea for us to get back together. He showed up to my house under the influence and in pain. Angrily, I opened the door yelling and asking him to never to show up to my house again. A few moments in, he began physically attack-ing me, and I was fighting for my life. I was unable to get to my gun. I blacked out for a few seconds and then when I came back I heard a voice. The first thing I heard was, "when in trouble call on Jesus." I whispered, "Jesus." The next voice I heard was, "tell him you're pregnant." I said to him, "so you're going to kill the baby and me." Instantly, he stopped. Then he said, "I don't give a fuck about you dying, but I wouldn't kill my baby." He left. I shut the door. After that, the next hours or minutes or seconds all became a blur. I went into shock. I came into consciousness completely wet, laying on my bed, shower still running, and saying the Lord's Prayer. In moments, I was able to collect myself, and I called the cops. While waiting, I thought he could've killed me and then I thought he'll never leave you or forsake you. This is one of my many defining moments. This one came with several unforgettable messages that changed my perspective forever. Above all else, I learned that the mind stores everything and will recall it when needed, whether you believe in the words or not.

Being attacked by someone you love or claims to love you will royally mess you up. You feel like you missed the signs. You want to shrink and hide. You're angry, embarrassed, hurt, disappointed, and vengeful. However, I understood that life needed to go on. This was when I had to rely on my Ego to save me and the way it was set up at the time did save me. I didn't know anything about affirmations. However, I knew I wasn't ready to die and that I wanted to be a boss. For weeks, I would get out of bed and say, "brush that shit off and get over it. You can't be his friend. It's not your fault. He has fucking issues." I had to make a daily commitment not to drown in my doubts and not waste away. Some days my voice wasn't enough and I had to get creative. On days I felt bad or "unpretty" I played my favorite songs on repeat. Awhile later, I opened up about my situation, and someone asked how I managed to push through. Also, they questioned how I went to work with a smile and continued to focus on my goals. Looking back on it, I think they thought I was lying because my behavior was different from anything that they had ever witnessed. As a result, they told me stories of others in my situation. These were stories of self-destruction, fear, promiscuity, and abuse. All the things I can't believe I dodged. They were looking for me to say something great but all I could say was, "I talk myself off the ledge every morning." Until I spoke the words out loud, I didn't realize it was a method to my madness. I hadn't realized I was speaking against what I felt. This was when I began to control and monitor my intake consciously. I realized the power of it all.

Everything you see, do, and listen to has some effect on your daily activities. Your eyes are a camera, and your ears provide the audio. Then it's your brain's job is to process every image and frame; subconsciously and consciously. What we choose to intake will be processed against our previous experiences, biases, insecurities, fantasies, and goals. Creating common themes within our thoughts and our actions. Those themes will show up in times we never imagined and immediate reactions we never suspected.

Think of everything like the juicy cheeseburger commercial or the song that gets stuck in your head. How many times have you found yourself craving a mouthwatering burger and you weren't even hungry, or you don't even eat meat? How many times did you sing a song that you don't even like? How is it that you have accepted this as the norm but think that other words and images are deleted from your brain? Not so. No matter how light-hearted, insignificant, or dumb as it may seem. Your brain is storing it somewhere. That's why it's important to choose your intake wisely.

Chapter Questions:

1. What recurring negative themes continue to play out in your head?

    _____

2. What activities do you believe influence those thoughts?

    _____

3. What impact does that have on your current goals?

    _____

Action:

1. For the next 7 days, complete a daily journal of all of your activities; include the music you listen to, conversations you have, books you read and shows you watch.

2. Remove any activities that encourages negative themes or confirms negative thoughts.

3. Replace those activities with items that affirm your goals and supports positive thinking.

Notes:

BE YOUR OWN BEST FRIEND

The most intimate relationship you must have is with yourself. There isn't anything wrong with wanting to surround yourself with great people who love you. However, reflection and alone time shouldn't make you feel lonely or afraid. You should love loving on you. You should be someone you would love to hang out with regularly. Understanding that you are awesome and you amazing. Granted, there are times you might like yourself a little more than others, but you have to be your own best friend. Your best moments will occur alone; reflecting on your purpose, passion, and priorities. That constant connection is necessary to make sure you remain at your best and achieve 360-degree success.

Self-awareness is the first step to greatness. It is all about owning who you are, what you've done, and how it continues to impact your life. A summation of your experiences is based on what you do; consciously and subconsciously. How can you secure your spot in the future, if you are unaware of your present? Also, how the past has influenced your present. Honestly, you can't. It's impossible to grow in peace when you are being haunted by pieces of your lesser self. You must identify where they dwell, why they're there, and what they're consistently destroying.

Any action that evokes an emotion is triggered by something learned or experienced. Nothing that you do is based on coincidence. Take the time to learn what is driving your emotions and how your emotions are driving you. Too many times we dismiss behavior that poorly represents us or disrupts our peace. Not realizing we may have internalized how others perceive us, harsh words spoken to us, or traumatic events.

Learning why you do what you do is an interesting and enlightening process. Some things are pretty apparent, but others require a professional. The first time I attempted to seek a "special friend," I only attended one session. I wasn't ready, and I couldn't figure out why this woman needed to talk about everything from 5 to 25. However, as I began to grow, I know I needed a "special friend" because there were certain cycles I needed to break and my emotions were all over the place. One of my largest issues was not wanting to be seen or being rewarded in public. As a child, I had a pretty big personality. I was assertive, theatrical, and an overachiever. As a result, many people assumed I was seek-ing attention. Granted those things caused me to get atten-tion, but it wasn't my motive. I simply was being true to how I was created and became jaded by the world. I learned attention was bad and that being me was too much for most to handle. Consequently, I became afraid to fully share me with the world because I didn't want the drama and constant conflict. This hurt my business and my personal life. There were times I needed help or should've shared my struggles, but I didn't. I acted paralyzed. Regularly, I have to push myself outside comfort zone and invite folks into my world. Each day, I have to remind myself to remain unapologetically me and to live out loud. Thanks to the process and my "special friend" I've been able to live my version of the American Dream.

People assume that you seek a psychologist or therapist because you're crazy or unstable. That's a myth. Different health professionals specialize in different things. You seek services to keep you from going crazy, make sure you have healed from life's events, or to get help with making major decisions. It can be anything from a rough childhood, a rough breakup, or surviving a primetime special. Also, loss or fear of losing. Then there is survivor's remorse or not living up to the potential of your family. As you can see, there is a host of things that may need sound objective advice. Therapy isn't a dirty word, and it can make a huge difference on how you view life.

You must go the extra mile to make sure your world remains healthy and balanced. That requires an active commitment from you and that commitment requires you, to be brave and ask yourself some pretty tough questions. Also, the ability to revisit the past to see how that impacts the present. It's all about understanding why you do what you do and how that impacts your present and future. Getting a clear understanding of who you are on a deeper level and work-ing through any challenges supports 360-degree success. Neglecting to do so, will eventually lead to your downfall and force you to be mediocre at best.

In order to get the life you desire, you must get still and be at peace within yourself while you're by yourself. Take a timeout from life's demands to enjoy your own company and to do you. Also, utilizing time to self-reflect on what has happened in your life up until this moment. It is the only way you will understand what's driving you emo-tionally and how those emotions are impacting how you lead your life. You will find that some things are easily figured out and some may require a "special friend". However, the experience can be enlightening and can positively change your world forever.

Chapter Questions:

1. How would you describe your current emotional state?

   _____

2. What makes you happy?

   _____

3. What makes you uncomfortable?

   _____

4. What makes you angry?

   _____

5. What causes you to shut down?

   _____

Action:

1. For one week record your emotions throughout the day. Document how you feel in the morning, mid-day, and before you go to sleep. Also, how you were spending your time during that period. Pay close attention to activities that cause joy, require a vent session, or cause you to shut down.

2. Find out what lies behind the emotion. Talk through it with someone who can be objective; whether it is a friend or "special friend". Remember this is to

gain clarity and understanding so take the time to listen and explain events that occurred in your life. If this causes a huge spike in your emotions, then seek the help of a professional. Most employers and health plans will contribute to a set number of visits or consultations. Treat this process like your future depends on it.

3. Commit to understanding that nothing you do is by coincidence.

Notes:

GAIN CLARITY

*R*emaining in a conscious and realistic state is everything. It is your responsibility to give yourself what
you require. It's not about making the time. It's about taking
the time. Everyone needs to reboot, reset, and recharge. It
should happen voluntarily and not due to a crash. Crashes
are painful, and the damage can be horrendous. Therefore,
you must learn to be still and be at peace. If not, you become
anxious, emotionally unbalanced, and you make decisions
that are not in alignment with your core.

Prayer and meditation are two proven skills that keep
you centered and seriously connected to your inner being.
It affords you a space that keeps you consciously in the
moment. It's not about being religious. It's about being
spiritually connected to the soul that resides in your body
because when it's at unrest then everything is at unrest.
Consequently, you engage in self-destructive behavior that
can potentially lead to long-term effects. Also, prayer and
meditation will prevent you from waking up in a space
where you are continuously doing but have no clue as to
why. Let's keep you connected to your purpose, passion,
and priorities, even if some lifestyle adjustments need to be
made.

Most people assume prayer and meditation are some intense processes that requires you to be more than yourself. Not so. Experts say, it allows you to become your higher self and I couldn't agree more. It gives you the power to channel your energy and tap into your core. This is the closest that many of us will ever get to being a ninja or bad ass superhero. I can't say you will be able to levitate, but you will elevate. It grants you the opportunity to gain focus and control in an indescribable way. I would be less of a human being if I kept this awesomeness to myself.

When I first began to meditate, I would put myself in a quiet space and focus on my breathing. It's not necessary to sit Indian style with your palms up unless you choose to do so. Initially, I would lie down, stand in a stairwell, or sit at my desk. What appeared to be random thoughts continuously crossed my mind. It was everything from what I wanted for dinner to things that happened several months ago. Over and over, I had to remind myself to focus on inhaling and exhaling, because that was the only way I could achieve stillness. I am naturally a busy body who is known to complete several tasks at a time, so, initially, it took a moment to relax and let go. It was a new way of life and a new way of thinking. Honestly, at times I wanted to quit. I remember saying things like maybe this isn't for me. Not because it wasn't for me, but I wanted to justify giving up. My feelings weren't connected to the activity, but I didn't want to address how the activity made me feel and what it made me realize. The consciousness allowed me to stay committed to myself and my goals. Then as time progressed the process became more intuitive and took less time.

Meditation and prayer are a power couple. They're great

by themselves, but they completely change your world when they're together. I would be doing you a huge disservice by recommending one without the other. There would be no way I could effectively pray without clearing out the clutter and checking my emotions. I learned when I do not meditate first, my prayers are misguided and they come from a place of anxiousness or frustration. Especially, if I am in a period of lack or need. Remember, I am naturally a bit impatient and need for things to be complete. The world never works on my timeline, so I am always forced to trust the process. Prayer is nothing more than talking with God. Some say God resides within them and others name high power. You can call on God, Allah, Yahweh, Buddha, or any other spiritual being. I am not here to argue beliefs or take a stance. I say, address it in a way that makes you better. The best advice I received about prayer, was not to get caught up in formalities but to outpour what's in your heart. Not be-cause prayer isn't sacred. Because people get so caught up in the process that they stray away from the purpose and what should be used to empower makes many people feel inferior. Years ago, I read an article that said to pre-tend like your closest relative is sitting in a chair and you are having a conversation, so that's I what I did. However, it wasn't t just any relative; it's one of my ancestors. Normally, I gave thanks for all the little things, asked for assistance with overcoming my challenges, and thanked him for knowing what I needed versus what I wanted. Also, to please allow me to see his work in all things. Over the years, my process evolved along with my faith. When not operating as my best self, I ask for forgiveness and mercy. Trust me, prayer time is prime time to be vulnerable and free. You can't pick a better space to cry, grieve, express frustration, heal and find peace. There are moments when I feel relieved instantly and feel a shift in my environment. However, you have to be open and have faith in the process. I am living proof that prayers are heard and answered. In due time, it all comes together.

My normal routine is to meditate then transition into prayer. Sometimes it may take 5 minutes and other times it can take up to an hour. It is usually dependent on what I currently have going on in my life. If something is troubling, angering, or grossly frustrating me, then it might require some extra time to get into my zone. However, I give my spirit and my core what it needs. When I don't everyone suffers, especially me. Take the time before you do or say something you might regret.

Remember it does not have to be an arduous process. Especially, if you are open and willing to commit. It might take a minute to find your rhythm, but it is necessary to remain in a conscious and realistic state. It ensures you are in tune with your emotions and prevents them from negatively hindering your relationships and your goals. More importantly, causing you to self-destruct. Prayer and meditation keeps you completely in touch with your core and enables you to achieve 360-degree success.

Chapter Questions:

1. What would be a good spot for you to conduct a meditation and prayer session?

   _____

2. What can you do to make sure you get uninterrupted time to yourself? Consider times when your house/office is quiet, will a sign help, or can you delegate duties to a family member/friend.

   _____

   _____

   _____

3. Does white noise or music make it easier for you to relax?

   _____

Action:

1. Carve out one hour to partake in a meditation and prayer session. Use your answers above to help choose the best (not perfect) place and time.

2. Remember to focus on inhaling and exhaling. Some find it useful to listen to white noise, which can be found via an AP or via nature (i.e., open window, running fan, water running, rain, etc.). If this is

your first time or you haven't completed a session in a while, schedule it towards the end of your day or when you have some free time. This allows you to enter into the process without feeling rushed or pressured.

3. Journal your experience. Include how you felt before and after. Also, your challenges and the duration of your session.

Notes:

_____

_____

_____

_____

_____

_____

_____

_____

_____

_____

_____

_____

_____

_____

_____

_____

_____

_____

_____

_____

MANAGE YOUR THOUGHTS

*P*erception matters. You can control, as well as dictate your thoughts. If you are always complaining, you shift away from the goal and allow yourself to be defeated by the problem. As a result, all of the energy needed to make shit happen goes into talking yourself off the edge. It's draining and counterproductive. You are giving away your power when you allow thought monkeys to do backflips and somersaults in your head; forcing yourself to be all over the place and worrying about shit that doesn't count. However, if you learn to control them, then you can point your life in the right direction.

Training your thoughts can be much easier than it seems. In the beginning, it may feel unnatural, but as time progresses, it becomes second nature. It is simply counter-acting your thoughts. PMS or Menopausal moments are an awesome time for a crash course. Men, ask your partner or favorite women when yours is on. Trust me they know. Go with me on this one. It provides consistent practice. I mean like every day for quite a few good days type of practice. Okay, I digressed. Here is what I do. I get out the shower, I stand in the mirror, and call this exercise "finding your angle". As I stand there naked, I find one thing about my body that I love, and I pose. Two children and two decades later that angle has changed. At one point it was Janet Jackson abs, then it was my legs. Later, I would hit a stripper pose to make my booty look bigger and then it was a side shot. Hell, at times it was just the one dimple in my right cheek. It's always about finding that one area that is amazing and projecting your focus. If you change your focus, then you can change your life. You can't afford to allow your ADHD or ADD to get the best of you. You have to be fully focused. Don't take your eyes off the light. Let it blind you. Bask in the glow.

I was taught to focus on the good via my mom's feet. My mom has the worst feet ever. Her feet underwent plastic surgery, and they still didn't look great. However, she always wore sandals and open toed-shoes. The event, crowd, or function didn't matter. If she saw a pair of shoes, she bought them, and she wore them proudly. As a kid, I didn't get it. Why would she want to showcase her atrocious feet? She was a woman who loved nice things, stayed classy, and always looked impeccable. However, she could care less about showcasing a flaw that could be easily hidden. I was confused. As a result, I would repeatedly ask her why and she would respond, "Well you can't have everything." As I grew older, this became one of my favorite mantras and points of reference. Every time I noticed a flaw, I would say, "Well you can't have everything." Not only physically, but in all areas of my life. In some areas you have plenty and in others never enough.

Creating mantras and words of affirmation is imperative to redefining your thoughts. Sometimes you need to say it out loud, but more importantly, you need to say it to yourself. Some thoughts never meet the surface, yet they never leave our mind. Every time I think "this will never work," I follow it with God is preparing me for something great. If I think that I did a horrible job, then I say, "Girl you were born to be a boss." This doesn't mean I think I am perfect or shouldn't work on my challenges. It simply means that I understand I am a work in progress and need to be kind to myself. When you redirect your thoughts, you begin to feel better and always see the light at the end of the tunnel.

Your experiences are directly related to your perception. In many cases, your experiences shape your perception, which is normally the downfall. It doesn't allow you to live in the moment and it will leave you searching and stressing over things that haven't happened. Things that you don't even know will happen. It takes you out of the present and turns you into a Ms. Cleo. You become the plaintiff, judge, and jury. Also, the crooked cop that made a case with no evidence. Stand strong and don't be a part of the system. Don't allow the conditions of your past life to impact your current happiness and your future happiness.

In order to change your perspective, you have to change the angle. Make a conscious effort to replace a negative with a positive. Immediately, interjecting when you feel negative thoughts invading your space. One thought easily becomes ten and they completely take over your brain. As a result, you must offer yourself alternative ways of thinking and get rid of narratives that disrupt your peace. Place things in the best light possible. Remove the dark sunglasses and open the drapes, so that you can see the light. It will guide you and put you in a happier space.

Chapter Questions:

1. What tough situation would you like to change in your life?

   _____

2. What makes that situation seem impossible or very difficult to happen?

   _____

3. What are you currently doing to complete that task or improve that situation?

   _____

Action:

1. Identify one positive in the situation above. If you can't find one then try harder.

2. Write down 3 statements that contradict your fears or concerns that it will not happen.

3. Place that paper in a convenient location. Put it on a mirror, desk, in your wallet, or in your bag.

4. Read those statements once in the morning, once at night, and whenever you need to be reminded.

Notes:

_____

_____

_____

_____

_____

_____

_____

_____

_____

_____

_____

_____

_____

_____

_____

_____

_____

_____

_____

_____

_____

TAKE IT

$\mathscr{L}$earning to shape your perception isn't only helpful for managing internal thoughts. It's critical for managing your relationships with others. Too often, people are taught that when others don't share favorable feedback, they are ill-spirited, jealous, or just downright mean. If you don't have anything nice to say, then you shouldn't say it all. Well, at least that's what we learned. Now, what happens when that information is true or can make us better? Do the same rules apply? Is that person considered toxic and worth purging from our lives forever?

Let's be real. You will not always be a fan favorite. There are instances when the perception you have of yourself will clash with the way others experience you. In those moments, it's not about what you want to hear, but what you need to hear to become better. What can you take away from the conversation to be stronger, braver, and more successful? It's less about likability and more about becoming a better you. Is what they're saying worth applying to your life because it suits your best interest in the long run? However, understanding the basis and the nature of the criticism requires a certain level of emotional maturity and openness. You can't get caught up on the messenger, become a slave of your ego, or live in your emotions. You must learn how to pull up your adult undies, stand there, take it, and apply the pieces that count.

In your heart, you can know a thing to be true, but it sounds so different when it comes out the mouth of someone else. How dare they rip off your clothes and expose you to the world? You question their intentions, motives, and approach. I agree some folks are tactless and crude. Also, others may be too direct for a delicate soul. Then there are times when it has nothing to do with the approach. It is all about what you are ready to handle and what you feel you can process. It's about being able to own your shit and sit in the moment.

Separate the message from the messenger. Don't kill them because you aren't ready to receive the message. The truth doesn't only hurt, but it burns down bridges. Nobody likes to be reminded of their challenges, shortcomings, or failures. Especially, when it is something you haven't found the courage to confront. It pushes you to a place of anger, resentment, defense, and petty. I am talking petty to the hundredth power petty. It becomes the time to attack the messenger and everything they've done wrong in life. However, deflecting doesn't turn the truth into a lie and doesn't attribute to your growth. It highlights your immaturity, and it leads to random failures. Sometimes you must push through your emotions to get the message. The messenger isn't always a know-it-all, hater, or a witch. Sometimes it is someone who truly has your back and willing to hold you accountable. That is your village. Those are the people you need in life to be successful. If you weed them out simply, because you don't like their feedback, then expect to be lonely and delusional forever.

I get it! Sometimes you want to earn your t-shirt and wear it under a heavy trench coat in the dark. In most cases, that t-shirt has already been worn. Someone may have paid a different price or purchased it from a different store, but they know what it feels like on their skin. They understand the cost of owning it, wearing it, and to not being able to take it off. However, you're so fixated on creating your own experiences you don't see the validity of learning from someone else's mistakes. Their primary purpose in life could have been to wear the t-shirt, so you wouldn't have to share their struggle or be affected by the fabric.

People are not placed in our life by coincidence. Everyone there has a purpose and the opportunity to teach us something new. The adage says, "Can a drunk not teach you how not to be a drunk?" Some people say he should clean himself up before he gives advice. I strongly disagree. I spent half of my life learning what I wanted to be by watching others model what I didn't want to be. If three drunks lined the streets, then I needed to know what they all had in common. That way, I could figure out how to avoid their situation. Also, what I needed to do differently to eliminate unnecessary misfortune. You don't have to allow their failures to shape your fears but serve as a blueprint that can be modified into something greater than you imagined. You never know what you and the drunk have in common, if you don't take the time to listen.

Listening can be hard. Especially, if you believe a conversation is invaluable or it's not what you want to hear. Remember when you were a teenager. You knew everything and nothing at the same time. You thought you were invincible. You thought you were the first to ever do a thing and the first to ever experience a thing. You know what sucked about that? People who loved you had to watch you fail because they knew you weren't ready to listen and receive their words. After so many attempts they let you figure it out for yourself and they no longer provided warnings. This is not the mindset you want to carry into adulthood. The older you get, the greater the risks, and the more you're capable of losing. Also, recovery doesn't feel the same. There is nothing more disheartening than waking up 10 or 20 years later and realizing you are the same person you were years ago. Making the same mistakes; left feeling bitter and abandoned.

In life, we all need accountability partners. People who don't care about stroking our ego and don't mind telling us the truth. Someone to keep us humble and honest. Someone who is willing to risk the relationship so that we can accomplish our goals. Sometimes they may take the form of a friend, mentor, boss, coach, or family member. If you are lucky, then you will have more than one. If you don't have one, then let's question why. Is it because you can't accept criticism or feedback? Is it because you've closed yourself off to the world? Maybe it's because listening and applying information is a challenge. It's not always about someone being intimidated by you or unable to handle your personality. Sometimes it is strictly about you looking for validation or preferring to be around those who are agreeable and willing to stroke your ego. Those who value surface level conversations and allow you to live in your reality. If you believe this isn't you then evaluate the last time you were provided with some feedback. Not just average feedback but that feel it in your gut, I can't believe you just said that, wait what happened, or well damn kind of feedback. The kind of feedback that takes your breath away and leaves you speechless. Often, it's not about what we say, but what we do. If we surveyed 100 people, 90 would say they value honesty and loyalty. However, if we took inventory of their lives, we would find the contrary. The truth about honesty is most people aren't honest with themselves.

Ability to walk in your truth and out of your ego requires everything we've explored so far. It's when living in a conscious and realistic state becomes necessary. Also, knowing no matter how hard it is to process the feedback that it's okay and to you must be kind to yourself, because it's not the end of the world and life goes on. You must continue to be open, committed, and fixated on all of the positive things, if you expect to grow. Accountability isn't a dirty word if the criticism allows you to excel and plummet to new heights.

It's so easy to believe that everyone who criticizes us is a hater and everyone who challenges us is a bitch. Too often, it has nothing to do with the messenger but our ability to receive the message. Many times, we discredit the message by pointing out the flaws of the messenger. However, there isn't any growth and reward in it for us. Attacking the messenger doesn't make their words less true or lend itself to our success. Whether we are at work or home, we must find people who hold us accountable. We need to push past our feelings and ego. All advice we receive isn't meant to be malicious. It can prevent us from failure. Time and oppor-tunity does not wait for anyone, so why live a life of regrets?

Chapter Questions:

1. Describe the last time you received unfavorable feed-back and it contained some truth.

    _____

2. Were you ready to confront reality?

    _____

3. Do you think it was delivered appropriately?

    _____

4. What did you learn from the feedback?

    _____

5. How can the feedback be applied to make you better?

    _____

Action:

Each time you receive unfavorable or harsh feedback do the following:

1. Ignore the messenger
2. Listen with the intention to learn
3. Determine if the feedback can you make you better
4. Apply the feedback if applicable
5. Thank the person for sharing their perspective

Notes:

_____

_____

_____

_____

_____

_____

_____

_____

_____

_____

_____

_____

_____

_____

_____

_____

_____

_____

_____

_____

Accept All of You

$\mathcal{M}$ost of us spend a significant amount of time in our ego. We desire to always see ourselves as our best selves, which is dangerous. You must be able to take the good with the bad. Therefore, be able to accept criticism and feedback as a tool to become stronger. Accountability and judgment get a bad rap. Accountability is the act of holding you responsible for your actions and how they can impact your life. Judgment is when you can draw a sensible conclusion. Both have a place in this world.

My father says, "If 100 people are all saying the same thing then there must be some truth behind it." Meaning, if people continue to tell you that you're abrasive, unapproachable, mean, or selfish, they might not be lying. Although your actions may not be malicious you have to question what drives those perceptions. What vibe are you sending to the world? What about you makes folks continue to misread or judge you? Are your past experiences being acted out in your daily roles? Their opinion isn't everything, but make sure that your intentions match your actions. Own who you are at all times and remain in a conscious and realistic state.

There is power in knowing who you are and being able to stand in your truth. Being able to scream it to the world without hesitation, regret, shame, or embarrassment. Having an ability to say what you've done, where you've been, and how you've changed in a way that empowers you and demonstrates your growth. Knowing yourself in the most intimate and vulnerable way enacts those superpowers, and it fuels your ability to conquer the world.

Most people would like to believe that what others think and say doesn't influence them. I'd beg to differ. The majority will accept the norms and others will reject those same norms just for the sake of being different. However, in both situations, the individual is being controlled by a standard set outside of themselves. As a result, many people live as a shell of themselves out of fear, judgment and rejection. They never learn how to establish their bar and happily live life on their terms.

Feeling like the black sheep or the odd man out can be daunting and forces you to question your worth. Also, it makes you believe that you are in constant conflict with yourself and those around you, but that stems from being uncomfortable with who you are. On average, people will say they don't care what folks say. They really don't mean it. Remember, anything that causes us to have a response or reaction has emotionally affected us on some level. Anger, rage, frustration, and annoyance are all emotions. When someone truly doesn't care, then they don't feel anything. More importantly, they don't feel the need to refute, rebuttal, or respond. They remain consistent and don't adapt their be-havior based on a role. They're not afraid to be silly, funny, or at times slightly inappropriate. They live life like they're dancing naked in the mirror.

Who are you? The single, hardest question for most to

answer. Fifteen years ago, I would have defined myself by circumstances and situations. I would have responded using my roles and titles. Then, I would have thrown in a few cliché' phrases suitable for an online profile. I was fearful that my faults would be judged and my insecurities would make me vulnerable. Therefore, I publicly acknowledged the person that I assumed most people could handle. The things that could make me a fan favorite and appear more amicable. This was way before I learned never to shrink, we all have strengths, and we all have weaknesses. Before I became unapologetically me.

Once upon a time, I led a workshop and lecture at an area high school. As a result, I shared many details of my life; including being a single mother, previous periods of depression, growing up in a broken home and my anger issues. At the end, a young lady approached me and asked how I could I share my story with strangers. She asked if I was afraid of getting judged or experiencing backlash. I explained to her that we all have stories and that our power is in our voice. If people talked more, they would realize we are all humans and face similar struggles. More importantly, we grow by accepting everything that has happened to us, owning our portion, and using those lessons to become stronger.

Somewhere we've been taught that acknowledging our flaws is a sign of low self-esteem and negativity, but if you can't be honest with you, then who can. We have to shift that narrative and see it as a source of strength and power. I was devastated the first time I had to stare myself in the face and admit my faults. I felt guilty for not fulfilling the dreams of a younger version of myself. I couldn't believe that I became so guarded, arrogant, and self-centered. Let's not forget, I allowed folks to become permanent fixtures in my life, because I was dragging the bags that I failed to unpack. Consequently, I made a list of all of the things I loved about myself and all the things I loathed. My eyes were wide open with tears streaming down and mascara smeared on my cheeks. I was overwhelmed and a mess. However, I knew I had to collect myself because my legacy was dependent on it. I used the things I loved as affirmation to balance the uncertainty.

How do you wake up one day and just change everything? You don't. It's impossible. You take it one task at a time. Then, you turn your thoughts into viable measures. You understand that as hard as you try, there will be moments when you backslide into old habits and you have to fight your way out. If you get stuck, then you can find a comfortable couch, lie on it, and get professional assistance. Remember, therapy changes lives and it isn't a dirty word. Also, change is an emotional workout. Before you get the opportunity to see the full benefits, it will hurt a little and leave you slightly exhausted. However, if you invest the time and energy, you will be able to reach new heights. Your awakening will allow you to break cycles, generational curses, and disrupt negative thinking. You can take your power back. Consequently, you won't live in your past mistakes or non-beneficial behavior. By the way, did I say therapy isn't a dirty word?

In this life, there are items that allow us to shine and others that dim our light. Knowing our strengths is great, but acknowledging our weaknesses is key to 360-degree success. People waste countless hours trying to hide their flaws and cover up their blemishes. Own it. Then determine if it is something you want to change or something you can live with without harming yourself or others. We should never be the last to see our imperfections and we should not be the last to acknowledge our imperfections. Once you acknowledge who you are, you have the right to tell you stories and strip the power away from folks with ill and malicious intent. There isn't a need to feel ashamed, embarrassed, or guilty about anything you've gone through or experienced. Also, who you are at this very moment. If there is something you don't like, you can fix it, and you can then move on. Don't allow yourself to be defined by it.

Chapter Questions:

1. Who are you?

   _____

2. What characteristics allow you to shine?

   _____

3. What characteristics dim your light?

   _____

4. What are the misconceptions people had about you?

   _____

5. What do you do that lends itself to that perception?

   _____

Action:

Contact two friends or family members and ask them the questions below:

1. What are your best attributes?

   _____

2. How do they experience you?

   _____

3. What can you change to support your growth and your goals?

   _____

Notes:

THE POWER IS YOURS

You have the power to decide what deserves your attention. The advice and recommendations of others are good and it should be considered. However, it is still your life and your rules. Living on someone else's path or in someone else's shadow isn't an option. You can't find solitude resting in someone's interpretation of who you are and where you are supposed to be in this life. You must know what isn't up for debate, what shouldn't waiver, and your own level of comfort. Just like you should know what's hindering your growth and aiding itself to your setbacks. You should have a clear understanding of where you are in life; the good, the bad, and the ugly. This is an ability to stand strong in your current goals and actions. This is not for the sake of your ego, but your ability to live in your truth.

You must remain in a conscious and realistic state when you're choosing where to focus your efforts. You must stay true to who you are and who you were designed to be. Failure to do so will put you on a road to nowhere. You'll be constantly wanting and expecting more, feeling unsatisfied in your purpose and unsuccessful in your life. No Bueno! Remain conscious and clear, because that clarity will enable you to follow your instincts and be real about who you are at your core. Also, it allows you to see what requires change as you commit to being greater and stronger than you've ever been before.

When I underwent my initial mental makeover, I had no clue on how to become, "the change I wished to see in the world." It was a great quote, but I didn't know how to apply it. Since Ghandi said it though, I had to make it work. I figured I'd just jump and then act. Then everything would fall into place. Initially, my actions were centered on being completely opposite of who I was at the time. It sounded like a great idea because my current state wasn't working. Therefore, I ran with it and I based my decisions on making the new Mel the polar opposite of the old Mel. That was a huge mistake. I was trying to rebuild Rome in a day while stripping away everything, even the things that didn't need to be fixed. As a result, it left me constantly challenging my instincts. I was completely confused and I lost my balance. I had to revisit what made me feel happy and productive. I was all over the damn place.

My Nigerian friends say, "Out of chaos comes opportunity." Oh boy, are they right? I found an abundance of jewels while trying to figure it out. Hell, while trying to figure me out. In the process, I learned I was created to be bold, assertive, and slightly fiery. That I was great with change and I didn't mind taking risks. That was who I was at the core. My core didn't need to change, it was how I used my core that needed to change. Have you ever heard someone say, "He's so smart but he just doesn't use it for the right things?" Well, that is how I was mismanaging my core. Therefore, I had to take a step back to make sure that my actions matched my intentions and all my characteristics were working together for my good. Therefore, I developed a system to allow me to classify and list out my priorities. I know you're not thinking of another system, but ideas are one thing in your head and something totally different on paper. Paper is your friend.

My system is basic but has proven itself as useful. Things don't have to be complex and overly thought out to be effective. Sometimes, less is more. How it works is that everything falls under three categories: the core, characteristics you're working on, and characteristics that you have no desire to change. The core is the most consistent category and normally drives the other two. Together, they are the basic building blocks to owning who you are, taking back your power, and exerting your energy towards what makes you better. This isn't a once in a lifetime exercise. The list will change and require modification as you grow and evolve.

The core is the most deceiving group. It's a thin line between how you were actually created and how you think you were created. You must mentally return to the place before you were jaded and allowed others to influence your actions. Your core is what you are unable to remove from your life without feeling completely lost and disconnected from your gut. They are those things that are intuitive and show up in all areas of your life. Common ways to identify your core is by evaluating your talents, examining things that are easier for you to achieve, and determining the balance you bring to any group. This is where your passion, purpose, and influence lies. Warning: just because it is a core characteristic doesn't mean you are handling it correctly. Most core characteristics can be used for good or evil. Think of the smart guy who grows up to be a drug lord versus a CEO. Many times, we interpret the output as the core characteristic. For example, we'll say he's a hustler or a go getter. That's the outcome. His characteristics are that he is persistent, determined, strategic, charismatic, and persuasive. Remember, you can't define yourself or others by the roles they lead. It's much deeper than that because we aren't one dimensional creatures. Also, the foundation of all of our actions, choices and decisions stem from who we are as people.

Next on the list is your list of required changes. This category is your work in progress and requires the largest portion of your time. You are acknowledging that something is an issue or concern. Also, that you are diligently working in that area to become better. There will be times you can change these things in 6 weeks and other times it may take 6 years. It varies. Your work in progress is typically related to mismanaging your core. For example, change is my friend and I am constantly seeking ways to advance in many areas of my life. Often, I am so eager to embrace change that I can become obsessive and a bit anxious when things are not moving at my expected speed. Anxiousness is something I continue to work on and it requires reminders at every turn, because it has been known to take me off task and change my course, prior to the plane getting off the ground. Unlike other things this has been a constant on my list. Yes, I've gotten better, but I am not free and clear. Honestly, there have been times that I questioned my ability to completely kick it. Then I remember to be nice to myself, because I'm human, at least most days. Perfection is an illusion. Therefore, each day I remain conscious and chip away at it. My hope is that you will do the same no matter what's on your list. Remembering that if it makes you better then you must commit to making the change. Don't let people make you feel ashamed or embarrassed about being a work in progress. We're all different but we all have issues. At least you're working on yours.

Lastly are characteristics you have no desire to change. The characteristics that you truly love about yourself, that contradict who you are at the core, or you don't think are that serious. You may not be sure if it's a core part of your personality but you know you can live with it being the same. For example, some people were born to be sensitive, so they are able to express empathy and provide the water to balance a world of fire. Some people might tell them to become tougher or more guarded. However, that would cause them to be in constant conflict with themselves and it does more harm than being their true self. Also, these can be the items that you have delayed because you feel like your time is better invested in other things. Over time, this list may require an update because the characteristic or behavior has become imbalanced and unhealthy. If that's the case, then you want to make sure it becomes work in progress. For now, you have determined you can live with it and the rest of the world will have to deal.

When it all comes together, you should be in a position where you've looked at who you are and be satisfied with the person you are trying to become. Also, the commitment you made to work through the process. Knowing your goals and shortcomings should provide a sense of freedom from the jail that may exist within your mind and the minds of others. You can only change what you acknowledge and what you've already acknowledged shouldn't give power to others to make you feel inferior or embarrassed.

We were all created differently and given core qualities that make us influential. Sometimes, it's not about changing those things but using them for the greater good. Ability to call out and classify your characteristics, gives you a clear insight of who you are and what work needs to be done if you desire to achieve 360-degree success. Also, it allows you not to feel threatened or defensive when other people point out your questionable characteristics, either it is something you are working on or not. When both are mentioned, you shouldn't get emotional because you are making a conscious decision on how to live your life under your rules.

Chapter Questions:

1. What are your talents or hobbies?

   _____

2. What is the balance you bring to any group?

   _____

3. What makes you feel at your best?

   _____

4. What characteristics do you believe assist you with questions 1-3?

   _____

5. Based off question 4, what are your core characteristics?

   _____

6. What characteristics/items do you need to change?

   _____

7. What are things you don't have any desire to change?

   _____

Action:

Develop an action plan to change the items listed under question number 6 (from the chapter questions above). Consider the following:

- Language
- Intake
- Behaviors
- Perception
- Daily Routines

Notes:

_____

_____

_____

_____

_____

_____

_____

_____

_____

_____

_____

_____

_____

_____

_____

_____

_____

_____

_____

_____

_____

_____

CURB THE DISTRACTIONS

*D*istractions are real. They come in various shapes and sizes. They don't discriminate. The bigger the goal, the bigger the distraction. Right after you escape one, another comes around the corner. It's dangerous when the distraction disconnects you from your purpose or passion. Distractions are not only physical but mental, as well. All don't appear bad, but are they bad for you? Will they negatively influence your goals and overall success? Will they turn you into a woeful wanderer or a willing participant in nothingness? Those are all questions you need to ask yourself when journeying the course of life. You must rid yourself off anything that doesn't support your growth and goals.

Don't downplay your distractions. You have to understand that nobody will know your weaknesses more than you and the devil. What distracts me may allow you to persevere and what allows me to persevere, may distract you? Meaning, the same situation can be presented to two different people and have two different outcomes. Therefore, use some of that alone time to reflect on your world and your current state. Do you constantly see yourself evolving? Be specific. If not, then determine what in your world has recently changed and has been able to monopolize your time, energy, and resources.

Think of your goals as uncharted territories. A land that has not been previously drilled or discovered. Everything is new. Some things may appear familiar but packaged differently. How long will it take you to reach your destination if you stopped to admire every detail? It's like having five days to drive cross country and stopping in every city to use the restroom. Impossible! You'll miss out on the important things because you were hanging out in feces infested stalls. No Bueno!

A distraction is a deterrence from your final destination. There are two types of distractions. Those that can be avoided and those caused by matters outside of your control. Believe it or not, you can attempt to plan for both. Mapping out your trip ahead of time and putting safety measures in place will limit mishaps, as well as time spent. This might be your first journey, but there are tons of information that can be accessed from others who have traveled a similar path. Take the time to study their successes and failures versus being the eager 16-year-old who was thrown the keys for the first time. Also, review the typical climate and other natural factors.

Mapping out the trip is all about goal orientation. Creating goals that can be measured and monitored is critical to 360-degree success. It will define your scope and your focus. If it can't be measured or monitored, then it is not a realistic goal. My favorite approach to tackling tasks is through goal decomposition. In this approach, you set a large goal which can be achieved through the process of satisfying smaller goals. The high-level goal states what you are looking to do and lower level goals are answering how you will get it done. An example of a high-level goal is to desire to travel from New York to California in 5 days. Based on research, the proposed route takes about 42 hours, if you travel nonstop. Also, you will be only one in the car. You will need to sleep, eat, use the restroom, and refuel the car. Also, you want to do some sightseeing along the way. As a result, your lower level goals are to travel at least 8.5 hours per day, sleep at least 6-8 hour per day, refuel every 4 hours, and use the restroom when you refuel. Also, you will sightsee in Chicago, Boulder, and Las Vegas, which are located on the traveled route. At any point in the journey, you can assess yourself to make sure you are on schedule or determine if the goals need to be reevaluated.

Putting safety measures in place is equally as import-ant as mapping out the trip. This involves everything from knowing what you require as the driver, understanding the car, and what may potentially go wrong on the course. This step will be based on previous experience and research. First and foremost, determine what you need to be protected on the journey. What needs to be in place to keep yourself safe, along with the things you care about the most? For exam-ple, what would be the repercussions of not spending this time with family and friends? How can you avoid potential losses? What normally would take you off course? Life is very similar to the cross-country trip. It's one thing to set goals, but there are also basic requirements, such as, bud-geting the right amount of time and resources along with knowing what it takes to preserve the sanity of the driver and repair the car, if necessary. This goes back to your daily routines and remaining in a conscious and realistic state. It would be foolish to drive when your vision is blurry and you wouldn't purposely remove air from the tire. However, you understand it's not uncommon to get tired or to get a flat tire. Also, you wouldn't want to exhaust your budget in one day. You would put parameters in place to minimize the potential damage to the car and the driver. Journeying through life isn't any different.

Understand when the distraction permanently disables the car or when it's placing you on a path that does not lead to your desired destination. Read the signs and follow them appropriately. Failure to do so is accepting that your destination is no longer a priority. Also, understanding that the further you move away from the mapped course, the harder it will be to find your way back. In order to get back on course, you will need to tap into additional resources and add additional miles to the trip. Your resources and time will then increase.

Chapter Questions:

1. What things often distract you?

    _____

2. What are the signs that you have been distracted or that
    you are in the process of being distracted?

    _____

3. How does it impact your goals or growth?

    _____

4. What actions do you take to avoid the distractions?

    _____

5. What do you need to get back on course once you have
    been distracted?

    _____

Action:

   On a piece of paper, write the following:

   1. I will no longer allow (insert all your known dis-
       tractions) to deter me from my goals or my growth.

   2. Put the paper in a safe place that can be recalled,
       when needed.

Notes:

Stick to Your Goals

$\mathcal{L}$ife constantly changes the world around you. Therefore, you need to keep up with the flow. To do so, you need to be constantly transforming, evolving, and purging. You need to set your goals, stick to them, and put parameters in place to check yourself. It doesn't have to be some elaborate process. There are quick tools and resources you can maintain to perform a quick self-check. Also, to make sure you stay on track.

My ADHD like personality and need to see progress has made me a master goal setter. Goals are necessary, but shouldn't completely sculpt every aspect of our lives. You must have some time to smell the roses and feel the air. Therefore, I am not one of those folks that obsesses over everything and makes everything a goal. You can't enjoy life if you are always micromanaging every freakin' detail. It turns you into a Nut Job who values process over progress. Save everyone who loves you and save yourself. Focus on the areas of your life that need organization and structure. Those large areas that play into your big picture. My favorite areas are finances, family, faith, and career.

Develop a running list of your goals. You should have immediate, short term, and long terms goals that you consistently strive to complete. Your goals must be measurable and tangible. You must set tasks that will enable you to feel a sense of accomplishment. Start where you are and build upon it. It's nice to dream big, but if you are unable to outline a path to get there, then you will become frustrated. If you do not have a job, then you probably shouldn't set a goal to travel to Paris and save five thousand dollars in 30 days. Cut the BS and be real with yourself. You don't have to trash the dream, but don't set it as a goal. It can't become a goal until it can be measured and you have some understanding on how to make it happen. First, you should set a preliminary goal to attain a lucrative position that will allow you to pay your bills and create a travel budget. That would make an increase in savings and trip to Paris as the long terms goals. Then, attaining a position would be the short-term goal. The immediate goal would be to apply for ten jobs per week. It is easier to start with the larger goal and then work backwards. When all the goals come together, they should equal the vision you have for life and yourself.

Consider who you are as a person and your current responsibilities when creating your master plan. It can be detrimental to checking off those goals and moving forward in life. When I meet with my business clients, understanding their roles, responsibilities, and weaknesses is necessary. I used to cosign setting goals they felt they could fulfill without consideration for anything else. Then, I realized that people will say whatever sounds good because their intentions were great. However, their intentions did not always match their reality. As a result, I incorporated a process that requires us to holistically evaluate who you are in your personal and professional life. Oh boy, it made a difference! It made business a little personal, but the success rate increased tremendously. It ensures that we are not setting goals that interfere with things they are unwilling to sacrifice or what they need to feel successful. If it is important for you to get your children up for school every day, then you wouldn't set a gym time of 6:30 am every morning. If you are easily distracted, then you shouldn't set your core work hours when everyone is at home. Sometimes, you need to get creative to work around things that normally lead to unfavorable outcomes or not being able to see your goals through. Make sure you are selecting choices that are more favorable for your personality type. I am not saying you need to look for an easy way out. All I am saying is that, the quickest way to your destination is the path of least resistance. It's a big difference. One is expecting to put in minimal effort and the other is understanding effort is required, so you need to be strategic.

It is so easy to set goals and forget about them. Especially, when your time and attention is in constant demand. Also, there is a theory that suggest that once you tell someone your goal, it satisfies the same part of your brain, as actually completing the goals. The people who tend to do more talking, end up not actually doing and their goals are often left unaccomplished. Personally, I feel it all goes back to persistence and commitment. You have to keep your goals close and remember why they were created and how they can influence your life. It sounds so easy, but at times it is so hard. You will need reminders. Hell, we all need reminders! Put those goals in a space that you frequent or where they can be whipped out in .001 seconds. At times, I have carried it in my bag, my pocket, or placed it on a wall. Do whatever works. My favorite thing to do is set the password on my computer that reflects my immediate goal. I have used Collegegrad0501, Homeowner410#, Boss2006$, Nobacksies!, and many more. Every time I applied this technique, I achieve my goal. To avoid tossing them to the side, they must remain relevant.

The whole purpose of making your goals tangible and measurable is to track your progress. There is nothing like working hard on a thing and not being able to see progress. Especially, when you are spinning it and flipping it in different ways, but you still have nothing more than a need to do better. Your immediate goals will allow you to set milestones and track where you are at all times. Then, once all of the minor items are checked off, you can cross off the long term or short term goal. There is such a rewarding feeling to know, "Oh shit! I did that!" It gives you a sense of pride, honor, and accomplishment. It becomes the momentum you need to keep going and move onto the next task. Don't kill your momentum. Set up a routine to check on your goals. It can be daily, weekly, monthly, or quarterly. It all depends on where you are in life and the time frame you give yourself to complete the task.

Goal setting is one of life's most valuable skills. It enables you to cut through the bull and develop a prominent course of action. However, it is only a goal if you can create a path to get to the desired destination. It has to be measurable. If you can't track it, then it's just a dream. Dreams are wonderful, but they are not goals. Also, be real with yourself and set goals using the path of least resistance. Don't create a struggle where one can be avoided. That doesn't mean the goal will be easy. It means you will be strategic and think about who you are as a person and your responsibilities when setting your goals. Then, when you check in on them, you'll be able to check them off in no time. Goals promote momentum and progression. We all need momentum and progression.

Chapter Questions:

Answer each question at a high level.

1. What is your current financial goal?

   _____

2. What is your current familial goal?

   _____

3. What is your current spiritual goal?

   _____

4. What is your current career goal?

   _____

Action:

Utilize goal decomposition to create plan to accomplish all your goals. See the example below.

Goal I: Save at least 2400 dollar in the next 24 months.

    A. Save 100 per month.

        1. Deposit $50 per paycheck to my savings account.

        2. Create a budget to monitor my spending.

        3. 3. Pack my lunch three times per week.

B. Complete the example by listing a short term goal.

1. _____

2. _____

3. _____

C. Complete the example by listing a short term goal.

1. _____

2. _____

3. _____

Notes:

Make Room

Once you have established your goals, then you have to get out of the way and make room for the blessing. At this point, you are completely cutting ties with everything and everyone that doesn't fit your vision. I will be honest, this part freakin' sucks. Sucks! Sucks! Sucks! I've been through this process several times and initially, it never makes me smile. There are people we definitely want to keep around because they provide a sense of stability and familiarity. However, you need to have a truth moment and understand they may not positively influence your growth. Keeping those people around is like saying you are comfortable trying to force what doesn't fit or flatter. We've all been there and we've all done it, but at some point, you have to choose you. Especially, when you are fighting for yourself and trying to maintain your identity and your peace. Sometimes even your dignity. Take a deep breath, connect to your center, and move them out of the way.

It's nice to think that everyone will support your growth. That folks would be happy for your development. But you need to be aware that strangers and friends alike will challenge you in unimaginable ways. It's unfortunate, but everyone can't handle your glow up and they won't know how to handle you. It might sound crazy because you will see yourself as the same in many aspects. However, your energy, vibe, and interests will be slightly different. As a result, the only friends you can grow with are the friends that continue to grow. The irony is that sometimes people think they are growing, but they're stuck, stagnant, and stifled. Not to mention, they are secretly aiding our downfall because they represent the things we worked so hard to overcome. It isn't that you believe you're better, but you are at a space where you want more.

Many times, we claim we are ready for success and ready to win, but are we? Have we prepared ourselves for all the haters, competition, and pressure? Are you prepared for all the folks that will be dying to be you and claiming you're not worthy? Too many people give up on their hopes and dreams because they are unable to handle the adversity. Often, we do not know how to respond when the hurt wears a familiar face. The people we expect to be there disappear into the corner and the ones we never imagine throw us a lifeline. People are a mystery and trying to understand their thought process will give you a headache. Focus on being great and trust that the Universe will send the right people at the right time.

Overtime, I have been called every adjective mostly applied to strong, assertive women. I've been called a bitch and a lesbian. I've been referred to as an Alpha and a man and a feminist and a butch and too many others things to recount. Granted, my balls are pretty big, but physically I prefer the parts God gave me. I don't think those parts need to be substituted because I don't fit into someone else's box or role. Nor do I think that it is my responsibility to explain to another human being why I don't want their box. I'm well aware of why I get called these things and what energy I bring to the room. However, this is a characteristic that lives in my core and that I am unwilling to change. It has helped me way more than it has hurt me, so it has to stay. I understand that I'll be judged. Also, the people that judge me in private may shake my hand in public and I have to be okay with that or choose to go crazy. I would like to say this has always been the case, but not so much. I've learned not to throw away all of my F's over time.

I grew up in a space where I was always the outcast. I looked different, I thought differently, and I wasn't willing to compromise my ethics. Externally, I appeared tough as nails, but internally, I've had some moments of insecurity. I was human as fuck. As a result, I wanted to be understood and a part of something. However, feeling anything but that took me on a bit of a rollercoaster. At one point, I wanted to make everyone think like me. Then, I wondered why I didn't think like everyone else. Lastly, I realized I was designed specifically for my purpose and my mission. I realized I had no control over anyone other than myself, so I should let it go. It took me a moment to realize and accept it. It took me a moment to sit in that truth and not allow folks to make me question who I am. Consequently, I had to refuse to live a life of depression and mediocrity. I accomplished way too much in life to just stop there. So, this skinny overachiever with a potty mouth and a checkered past put in some work and stepped in her truth. My prayer is that all of you do the same. There are so many opportunities and life to be lived to focus on a hater. These are people who purposefully try to tear you down to boost themselves up or go above and beyond to taint your image.

You have to know that what is for you is for you. That the only person that can stop you from advancing is you. Sounds cliché, but the shit is true. It doesn't mean folks won't try because they will. However, you do not have to acknowledge them. Greatness speaks for itself. As long as you own who you are, be consistent, remain conscious, and play your lane. Then, you become unstoppable. You have to know it and act like you know it. Channel 10% of your inner Ye and expect greatness, despite many whispers and back door conversations.

Don't participate in activities that yields itself to doubt and speaks to your insecurities from a place of malice or ill-intent. Stay the hell out of the comment section of your social media pages. Block the person who constantly belittles you; in real life and in a virtual world. Choke the person who always shares with you the latest gossip. Okay, you can't choke them. I just wanted to make sure you were paying attention. Stop letting those folks pass messages and feed you their messy meals. As the old phrase goes, when people show you who they are, then believe them. You are not the exception to their rules. If you listen long enough, they will share how they think and handle others. As a result, you should never set up a comfortable space for folks to take you into character and tap into your worst self. Understand your triggers and avoid them when possible. Pay attention and know when to walk away. You can't give people the power and the resources to overthrow you from your throne.

Energy never lies. If your gut tells you that they're shady, then they're shady. At the very least, they aren't the person you should place in your intimate space. Remember, everyone's actions don't match their intentions. Therefore, don't be fooled by air kisses, fake hugs, and overly exaggerated affirmations. One thing life has taught me is that you truly don't know who's in your corner. Objects are not as they appear and neither are people. That's why we have instincts and they always tell us when something isn't for us. Then, sometimes we play stupid because of who they used to be or who we want them to be in life. Stop ignoring the backhanded compliments, side eye, eye rolls, and manufactured support. Know when to fall back or clean the house. Trust your gut.

Some say it's lonely at the top. I say not really, if you know how to clean the house at the bottom. You have to make room for who is supposed to be in your space. These are folks that are traveling up the same mountain. Those people will never come into your circle, if your entire team looks like a liability. Imagine you are trekking up the mountain, fully geared up, and on a mission. You have food, shelter, lights, and a plan. Then, you come across a person that looks like you, but they are carrying 10 other folks. Folks that look like what you've left behind or who you don't want to associate with at all. Folks that are not even prepared for the trip. The entire situation looks like a liability. You wouldn't want to deal with the complaining, sacrificing your stuff, or risk returning to the bottom. Understand everyone isn't meant for the trip and be okay with that. You can always love them from a distance.

People send negative vibes and ill-thoughts for a number of reasons. Sometimes it's about you, sometimes it's about them, and sometimes it's about you and them. The more you change, so will your circle. In a perfect world, everyone is happy for you. But we don't live in a perfect world. It sucks and people can be very disappointing. However, if you expect to grow, then expect to be hated, not by everyone but some people. Purge yourself from negative energy and people. That is the only way you can get what you deserve. Say it with me, bye haters!

Chapter Questions:

1. What do you and your closest friends all have in common?

    _____

2. What perceptions will others make about you based on your circle?

    _____

3. Who are your closest friends and do they support your growth/future?

    _____

4. What ways do your friends positively impact you?

    _____

5. What ways do your friends negatively impact you?

    _____

Action:
Evaluate your friendships and remove anyone that is toxic to your future from your intimate space.

Notes:

Move On

*P*eople do fucked up things. If you are waiting for a person to admit their wrongs and apologize, then you might be waiting awhile, if not forever. Truthfully, most people don't recognize when they are fucked up and consistently hurt others. For them, it is business as usual and often, a series of events caused them to be in an unhappy place. At some point, we've all been that fucked up person. We have fallen short, failed somebody, or our actions didn't match our intentions. However, when it's us that has been broken or let down, we forget what it's like to be the defendant versus the plaintiff. We measure the severity of our actions differently, but there is at least one person we cut with a machete' versus a butter knife. However, you can't let someone else's actions or lack thereof hinder your growth and success. For that to occur, you must not take their actions personally. Learn to find peace within yourself, and vow to be great despite your past.

One of the hardest things to do is not to take someone's actions personally. Especially, when it is someone who was supposed to protect, provide, or support us. A person that we have trusted and has taken up an intimate place in our lives. However, I've learned that people treat you poorly due to three things: fear, pain, or conditioning.

The Fearful: They are always in protection mode and they're also terrible communicators. Instead of telling you why they are upset or why they feel out of control, they divert attention from the core issue and deflect. As a result, it's easy for small arguments to turn into WWWIII. They tend to ghost and give up relatively quickly because they are scared of getting hurt, repeating cycles, and feeling used.

The Hurt: Constantly repeat cycles within their lives. They normally don't know how to heal or recover from the ill ways of the world. They normally misdirect their anger, pain, resentment and disappointment. Emotionally, they're all over the place and you become a casualty in the war against themselves.

The Conditioned: Old dogs performing old tricks. Often, they want to be different and do things differently, but they don't know how to be different. Change is hard because they've spent a lifetime living in dysfunction. They'll accept things as it is and rule out being any different. Even if they decided to change, you will see glimpses of the past for quite some time.

All these three categories of people have absolutely nothing to do with you as an individual. It's all based on their personal experiences, failures, and upsets. In life, we can all experience situations that can take us out of our natural element. Happiness is contagious and you can't fake it. If a person is consistently treating someone poorly, then they are fighting their own internal battle. Most people wonder why someone would treat them poorly, if they know what it feels like. Most of the time, it is because their behavior has become embedded in their thinking and daily routines. You can't tell a bird born with a broken wing what it feels like to fly.

You must free yourself from all the lies. Every story that you told yourself about their behavior must be released. Too often, we sell ourselves a story that is never vetted or validated. For example, if they loved us more, valued our relationship, or held us as a higher priority, they wouldn't treat us in that manner. Stop carving out space in your head to devote to the unknown. You don't know why your mother chose to get high every day or why your daddy wasn't more involved. You don't know why that man always cheats or can't seem to provide. You don't know why you never felt good enough for her or why she continuously yells. It's not your problem and you do not have to own it. Get to a place that makes you feel empowered and heard, but not with the expectation of an apology. Your only expectation should be to release your feelings and start your healing process. Remembering that process is different for everyone. For some people, it will be to confront the person that did them wrong. Others may need to see a special friend (i.e., therapist). Some people can move on after they write a journal entry or poem. Honestly, I've done all of the above because I refused to carry any baggage or let anything stop me from being great.

You must be a victor and not a victim. You have to make a commitment to be the best you can and that only comes when you push past your past. Before I knew what I wanted to be in life, I only knew what I didn't want to be. I never saw an example of the woman I envisioned and the examples that were close felt out of reach. What I did know is that, I didn't want to get stuck in a little town with big city dreams. As a result, I was constantly challenging myself to learn new things, push the envelope, and step out of my comfort zone. There are times I felt overwhelmed and extremely unstable because I was entering new territory and constantly being the student. There were people I thought were here for a lifetime but they were seasonal. I have endured every type of pain you could possibly imagine. I've been abandoned, abused, and taken for granted. My reputation has been slandered and jealous friends struck. At one point, I didn't read urban fiction because it felt too much like my life and I didn't like the ending. I decided I wasn't a basic kind of girl, so I wasn't going to get stuck in basic ass life, fulfilling someone else's goals, and living out someone else's dream. I'll be honest there have been times I thought it was easier, but every time I tried, life forced me to be honest. Teaching me that I needed to stay true to my path, but to do that, I need to forgive all of those who had hurt me.

The act of forgiveness is liberating and extremely complicated. There is nothing like talking yourself into forgiving people you don't feel deserve your forgiveness. Just accepting that you'll forgive them takes you through a plethora of emotions. You revisit what they've done, you curse them in your head, you decide it's not worth it, and you make it all about them. Thinking how can this be a good idea, then you determine that your forgiveness should be their gift and if they do not respond correctly, you'll write them off forever. You're upset and mad just at the thought. It's crippling and debilitating. It makes you the fearful, the hurt, or the conditioned. It turns you into them. Let that shit go.

I know you are thinking it's easier said than done. I'm thinking that phrase is for folks that don't really want to get it done. Get clear and stay conscious. Be honest about your emotions and release them in meditation and prayer. This session probably will be a little longer than normal, but your future and healing depend on it. You can't get caught up in things that haven't been vetted and validated. The more assumptions you make, the more you will talk yourself out of the process. You don't know their truth or how they truly feel. Honestly, you don't even know if they are ready to share or be honest with themselves. No matter how they respond or what they may fail to acknowledge you can't take it personal. Forgiveness is about you and dropping off those heavy ass bags to spare your back.

My current reality doesn't match my current vision. It matches the vision I had for four or fourteen years ago. Once you make a commitment to yourself to be great, you will constantly evolve, seek greater, and become greater. However, part of that process will require you to refuse to take ownership of the issues of the broken, learn how to release any negative feelings, and renew your spirit. Most importantly, to forgive and release. Not for them but for you. If not, you become the same person that have hurt you. Committing to greatness changes your perspective but doesn't stop life from happening. However, don't let anyone's actions stop you from being great and receiving everything life has to offer. Don't become the broken bird. Be at peace and move on.

Chapter Questions:

Think of a time when you were the defendant not the plaintiff.

1. What did you do?

   _____

2. Was it your intentions to hurt the other person?

   a. If so, what was your motive?

   _____

   b. If not, what was your emotional state?

   _____

3. How did you feel about the person you hurt?

   _____

4. How did the person respond to being hurt?

   _____

5. What assumptions did they make about you and your actions?

   _____

Action:

1. Make a list of all the people you need to forgive.

2. Mentally prepare yourself to forgive them.

3. Understand this is about your progression and not their ability to do anything different.

4. Understand you don't need them to accept, acknowledge, or ask for your forgiveness.

5. Write a letter, journal entry, or have a conversation that informs the person what you forgive them for and how their actions have made you feel. You don't have to share it if you're not comfortable.

6. It's a new day. Let it go and commit to moving forward.

Notes:

_____

_____

_____

_____

_____

_____

_____

_____

_____

_____

_____

_____

_____

_____

_____

_____

_____

_____

_____

REMOVE THE COVERS

*Y*our greatness is hiding behind your fears. You have to take several deep breaths, dig through the layers, and get what you deserve. Growth is scary. It makes you question everything you thought you knew and what you assumed was working. However, through each experience and lesson, you are being pushed to do more and be more. You're given the clue to answer a calling that is greater than you fully imagined. Answering this question appears to be the impossible. Once you pick up the phone, then what do you do next? It's the age-old question that we've all had to answer. The thought of the unknown makes us uncomfortable but don't be defeated. Do the uncomfortable.

There is only one way to conquer fear. You have to look the monster dead in the eye, scream your favorite obscen-ity, and tackle it head on. However, you can't expect to overcome the beast you claim doesn't exist. Acknowledge it and the power it has over you and your actions. Then size it up and strategically attack. No moment will be the right moment, so take several deep breaths and just do it. Go for it. Take complete control.

The root of all of our fears begins with a story. A story

that we've told ourselves to protect us from hurt or disappointment. A story where we have allowed ourselves to be a victim versus a victor. We start off thinking we are going to fail and that we are going to fall. Conquer those thoughts and step away from the bridge. Stop drawing conclusions on your new chapter. Create a new story. Act on your desires, your passion, and your purpose without adding a tragic ending. Be in the moment and expect nothing but greatness.

The negative is easier to accept because it causes the most trauma on our psyche. Our mind stores all of our extremes. The happy moments we wish to recreate and the tragic moments we try to avoid. The catch is that most of the tragic moments were unavoidable and life was just taking its course. We get so caught up in conquering the past that we don't live for the now. We don't live in the moment. Therefore, we give away our power to things that we're unable to change or control instead of ceasing the moment and shaping our actions into the life we deserve. You can't go backwards. You can't change people. You can't change what's in the past. What you can do is make sure all of your power and energy is placed into sculpting a beautiful life. A life that you deserve.

The number one thing holding most people back is fear. Fear of opinions, fear of failure, fear of reality, and fear they can't handle what's next to come. People spend more time obsessing over the fear than confronting it. Not confronting your fear is like hiding under the covers. That blanket can't protect you and it doesn't change the world around you. Anything that wanted to "get you" can, so what's the purpose? How long will you hide under the covers before you get the gull to tackle it head on? Come up with a strategy and choose not to be defeated.

I have dedicated my entire life to helping people conquer their fears to get to the next level. There is something amazing that happens when you step out of your comfort zone and conquer what you thought was impossible. Finding out the monster you have been dreading was just a shadow in the dark. That the only thing that has been holding you back is you. It's AMAZE BALLS. I have the opportunity to watch dreams come true and lives change forever. Not only for my clients, but everyone around them. It's funny how one person can be the catalyst of change for the entire environment. You never know who is watching and taking notes. So many people will watch our lives in silence and become secretly inspired.

It's unrealistic to think that you will never have fears. Who hasn't been knocked down or fell on the mat? Who doesn't have the demon lingering in the corner? Who the hell wants to fail or be disappointed? Only a narcissist thinks they are greater than all things. However, when you are afraid and do it anyways, the Universe begins to open up in an indescribable way. You become a freakin' super hero because you understand that everything is in your reach and nothing is impossible. You begin to take risk and go to places others may be afraid to go. Your possibilities are endless and so is your growth.

The person you see in the mirror is more than enough to get you to the next level. It doesn't matter what you've experienced or haven't experienced in this moment. You are your own super hero, vampire slayer, goal crusher, conqueror, and protagonist. Own it and believe it. Mediate, pray, and trust your gut. You'll have everything you need when you need it. Know that you're dope and expect dope things to happen.

Make a decision to do all things that make you uncomfortable and instantly provokes fear. There lies a victory that will take your life to the next level. There is no such thing as a little vision. If you see it, then know that it's yours. Don't allow fear to speak to you and trick you into thinking that what you see is impossible and that it's not for you. You need to inhale and exhale, stare it dead in the eyes, and slay the beast. Silence the negative thoughts through your actions. Believe that you can win and don't allow yourself to get caught up in a story from the past. Greatness awaits you! Put your middle finger up to your fears and do the uncomfortable. Victory is waiting on the other side.

Chapter Questions:

In terms of your growth and success.

1. What is the one thing you have been delaying due to fear?

   _____

2. What is at the root of your fear?

   _____

3. What experiences have enabled those fears to continue to grow?

   _____

4. How could tackling that fear positively change your life?

   _____

5. What can be a first step to addressing your fear head on?

   _____

Action:

1. Make a commitment to confronting your fear.

2. Pray and meditate.

3. Don't be afraid.

Notes:

SATISFY YOUR HUNGER

We continuously transform and evolve. As we grow, so does our hunger and we should prepare a plate that leaves us satisfied and fulfilled. However, that plate has to be prepared for us and by us. We are the only one who truly knows what we desire and what we need in that moment. Over time, we develop a richer palette and our body can no longer handle meals without substance. It is our responsibility to make sure we are properly nourished and not partaking in empty calories. What we were able to tolerate in the past now becomes obsolete. Therefore, we must make the necessary changes, decisions, and choices to satisfy our hunger and remain fulfilled.

In my earlier years, I survived off carbonated beverages and fast food. My struggle meal was a slice of pizza, a sugary soda, and a candy bar. Then, there was nothing like a trip to McDonald's before the club and a trip to Taco Bell after the club. It required little money, time, and effort. At the time, I didn't care if I was hungry within the hour. It satisfied my hunger for the moment and it allowed me to keep going. Also, it soaked up all the alcohol but that's a story for another day. Somewhere down the line, I was unable to process those meals. I would try but I would instantly become irritated and uncomfortable. My body began protesting and rejecting it. Telling me I was getting older and that I needed more. If I wanted to be happy then I needed to do things differently. As a result, I began to go to new places, try new things, and seek a new regime. I needed to be open and obedient. Nonetheless, I became persistent in my pursuit, because sometimes what I tried simply wasn't good enough or didn't agree with my system. You are not any different than me. If you continue to live and grow, you will no longer be able to tolerate processed meals that were inorganically created and not effectively built to fuel your system.

There is nothing like the conversation where you sit down as a group and try to decide what you want for dinner. People place a larger emphasis on where they want to eat versus what they want to eat, which increases their hunger and delays the meal. Most folks are inclined to state what they don't want versus what they do want; due to fear of rejection or simply not being in tune with their current desires. What would happen if we operate in our truth and proclaimed what we wanted? What would happen if we unapologetically state what we were hungry for in that moment? Best case scenario, the person serves as a valuable resource and will assist us with getting what we desire. Next case scenario, we decide to eat alone because the person is craving something different. In either scenario, it is up to us to make sure our needs are met. Frequently, people choose the needs of others over their own hunger. As a result, they end up with a meal that leaves them dissatisfied and unfulfilled. Also, blaming the other party for their poor choice, as if they were unable to choose something different. You always have a choice, even if that choice is to go into the kitchen, find a recipe, and cook your plate to order.

Once upon a time, I felt like my life was going in a different direction than I expected. Recently, I had a baby. My 9-5 was monopolizing my time, and I was suffering from postpartum depression. I was redefining my existence while trying to hold onto the pieces of me that worked. Every day, I woke up and had to recommit to being great and undefeated. It's the only time in my life that I couldn't plan and couldn't figure out what I needed to do next. Everybody else's voice lived in my head and I was turning my stereo up to constantly drown out the noise. I completely took it back to the basics. I needed to figure out what caused all of the magic to happen in my life and I needed to evaluate the times that I was most successful. I realized it was when I tapped into my core and made my seat at the table. In addition to preparing my own meal, trusting my gut, and saying fuck that salad, I need to eat steak. Not because it was trendy, but because salad didn't satisfy my hunger. I was a starving tiger. During this timeframe, other people tried to step in and help but they couldn't gauge what I craved in that moment. Nothing they produced was good enough because they've never seen me in this state. It had to come at a time where I was capable of articulating what I needed. I had to tell them exactly what I wanted or determine how their strengths could assist me. Also, be comfortable with doing it myself if they were incapable of helping me. I had to learn how to feed myself again and know that I was more than capable of serving what I needed. However, anything on the table had to be high in quality and nutrients. Fast food wasn't an option.

Consistently remaining nourished takes time and preparation. Also, it requires you to understand what it takes to feel fulfilled and satisfied. No two bodies are alike and no two people are alike. Therefore, you must know how to prepare your own meals and set your own table. The things you require will evolve as you evolve. Growth entails developing a richer, substantial palette because at some point, instant gratification won't do and you will be unable to digest rubbish. It will be intolerable and make you extremely uncomfortable. Your choices will not always be respected by masses. Your tasks may conflict with those around you, which may leave you at the table alone, but you will survive and you will make it. You will evolve into something beautiful.

Chapter Questions:

1. What do you require to relax, recharge, and reset?

   _____

2. What are you currently craving in your life?

   _____

3. What are you doing to satisfy your craving?

   _____

4. What will it take you to feel satisfied?

   _____

5. What can those you love do to support you?

   _____

Action:

Have a conversation with your close family/friends explaining the support you need to satisfy your current hunger or goals.

Notes:

HAPPY NEW YEAR

*R*emain mindful that you have control of your thoughts, words, and actions. Therefore, don't let anyone tell you what you can't do. Not even you! It doesn't have to be a new year to do new things. Sit down, record everything you plan to accomplish, and go get what's yours. It is truly that simple. Your happiness and success are closer than you think. That reoccurring thought or dream is connected to your purpose, so you owe it to yourself to make it a reality. People who constantly feel stuck are not moving in the direction of their purpose. You only have one life to live. You have the tools, so own it! Remove the distractions and place one foot before the other.

If you were given only a few months to live, then what would you have wished you made the time to do or get accomplished. Those are the things you should focus on. Those are the things you should be doing today. Those are the things that matter the most to you. Also, that is where your regret will live if you do not focus your time and energy appropriately. As a result, you must learn NOOOOOOO isn't a dirty word and everyone can't be there for your journey. It's nice to consider perceptions and opinions, at times. However, when those opinions or people take you off your path, then it's time to leave them where they stand and not feel guilty about it.

You already know any and everything can be a distraction. Act like it. Don't live in embarrassment, guilt, shame, failure, bitterness, and regret. What isn't for you is simply isn't for you. All things will not always work out as expected. You must remain clear and conscious, so you can see what a blessing is and what is trying to support your greater good. Upsets don't require a production and theatrical performance. Meditate on, pray on it, and trust your gut. Then count your blessings and note your lessons. Again, if something were to happen to you tomorrow, you wouldn't want anything that brings you pain or discontent to be connected to your legacy. So, stop chasing those negative things and channel that energy towards what is essential to your success and your happiness. Perception matters and ultimately, you have the final say on what gets your attention. It's your life and your rules.

It is never too late to get started and take your first step. Do it even when you're afraid and sometimes do it alone. No matter where you are in life, don't count yourself out or sell yourself short. As long as you are breathing, then you have a chance to overcome any obstacle. Start small and work your way up to the bigger things. If you light a match, I guarantee you will start a fire and over time, that fire will continue to build. Especially in areas that are known to be dry and were formally deserted. You want to open a daycare, then work on taking a few courses to get certified. Your bank account is low, then figure out what bills or expenses to cut (something always can be reduced). If you want a better position, then go back to school, and create a career path or network. Speak your vision. Some folks will say don't share your dream with others, I say speak it, claim it, and watch God align your life with the right people. When you are dream chasing and goal digging, you need a tough skin. Tough skin is developed through hard battles and sneak attacks. There are times you have to affirm yourself, dust yourself off, and keep pushing. I promise, if you are walking in your purpose, that right when you want to give up, you will get a sign to keep moving. Just be smart enough to listen and follow the signs. You got this!

This is your year, your day and your moment. Get out of your way. Then move everything else that is in your way. Sometimes, we are disappointed that things don't go as planned or expected, but just know that nobody can take what's yours... Don't take it personal. Keep moving! You do not have the time to cling to things that don't make you successful or happy. You want your legacy to be written in a way that speaks to your passion and our purpose. However, that can only happen if you keep moving towards your goals. Get yours and don't take no for an answer, unless it comes from God himself. Then you pray, meditate, and wait. Regardless, always make the choice to be great and the commitment to put yourself first. Happy Freakin' New Year!

EPILOGUE

Thanks for reading. It is my hopes that you will be able to apply all you've learned and know to achieve 360-degree success. Hopefully, you have made the choice to be great and you are committed to place yourself first. I can't guarantee you both will always be easy. However, if you remain diligent you won't regret your decision and the world around you will appear drastically different. Remember, once your perception changes then so will your life.

We all learn from each other's perspective and experiences. I would love to hear all about your journey, success, and how you were able to apply the lessons from the book. Please feel free to communicate with me at melbcook.org. In the meantime, don't forget to live by Life's 7 Critical Choices.

LIFE'S 7 CRITICAL CHOICES

1. Choose to Love Yourself Unconditionally
2. Choose to Get Over the Bullshit
3. Choose to Stay Positive and Productive.
4. Choose to Remain Clear and Conscious
5. Choose to Own Everything In Your Life
6. Choose to Never Be Defeated
7. Choose to Be Great.

Notes:

Notes:

Notes:

Notes:

Notes:

Notes:

_____

_____

_____

_____

_____

_____

_____

_____

_____

_____

_____

_____

_____

_____

_____

_____

_____

_____

_____

_____

_____